# CONTENTS

Samuel Serves in the Tabernacle ..... 4

God Speaks to Samuel ..... 6

The Ark Is Captured ..... 8

The Return of the Ark ..... 10

Saul Is Made King ..... 12

Saul Sacrifices Wrongly ..... 14

Jonathan's Bravery ..... 16

Samuel Anoints David ..... 18

David and Goliath ..... 20

The Friendship of David and Jonathan ..... 22

Saul Tries to Kill David ..... 24

Jonathan Warns David ..... 26

Abigail Shares Her Food ..... 28

David Spares Saul ..... 30

Saul Dies in Battle ..... 32

David Becomes King ..... 34

David Captures Jerusalem ..... 36

The Ark Is Moved ..... 38

# David Is Kind to Mephibosheth

Hannah was so happy with her new son. For a long time she could not have children. Then she had prayed, asking God to give her a son. "If You do, I will give him back to You, to serve You all his life," Hannah promised.

Now Hannah had her son. And she remembered her promise to God. The year after Samuel was born, Hannah's husband, Elkanah, went back to Shiloh to worship at the tabernacle, God's house. His other wife, Peninnah, went too, with her children. But Hannah did not go.

"Let's wait until Samuel is weaned," she told her husband. "Then I will take him to God's house and leave him there with Eli to serve God."

"We will do what you think is best," Elkanah told her. "Let God's will be done."

So Hannah stayed home at Ramah until Samuel was weaned. Then she and Elkanah took him to Shiloh, to leave him with Eli to serve at God's house. Samuel was still just a little boy.

"Do you remember who I am?" Hannah asked Eli. "I prayed here at God's house that He would give me a son. He answered my prayer, and gave me Samuel. Now I am giving him to the Lord to serve Him the rest of his life."

Hannah left Samuel at the tabernacle to serve God. Then Hannah prayed a beautiful prayer. "I am filled with joy because God answered my prayer," Hannah prayed. "No one is as holy as God. He feeds the starving people and gives children to those who cannot have them."

After that, Hannah returned home to Ramah with her family. But the boy Samuel stayed there at the tabernacle with Eli to help Eli do God's work.

# Children's All-Time Favorite Bible Stories
# David and Goliath
## Peter Pan Talking Books

**David and Goliath** and 17 More All-time Favorite Bible Stories from the Old Testament

Peter Pan

V. Gilbert Beers and Ronald A. Beers

## A Peter Pan Talking Book

Below every story there is a QR code linked to the audio recording of that story. Use your phone or camera to scan the QR code to hear the word-for-word audio.

*David and Goliath and 17 More All-time Favorite Bible Stories from the Old Testament*
Copyright ©2020 Inspired Studios, Inc. All rights reserved.

Published by Inspired Studios, Inc, Boynton Beach, Florida 33473

No part of the publication or recording may be reproduced, distributed, or transmitted in any form or by any means, including photocopying, recording, or other electronic or mechanical methods, without the prior written permission of this publisher.

ISBN 978-0-7396-1489-1

# God Speaks to Samuel

When Samuel was still a little boy, his mother, Hannah, gave him to the Lord. She brought him to the tabernacle, God's house. Samuel became God's helper, and a helper for old Eli, the priest, the man in charge of the tabernacle.

God did not speak often to people in those days, so what happened one night to the boy Samuel was quite unusual. This is the way it happened. Eli, whose eyes were getting dim, had gone to bed. So had Samuel, who slept in the holy inner room of the tabernacle where the ark of God was kept. Suddenly God called to Samuel.

"Samuel! Samuel!" He said. Samuel thought Eli had called, so he ran to see what he wanted.

"Go back to bed," Eli said. "I did not call you." This happened three times.

"If God calls you again, say that you are listening," Eli told Samuel.

When Samuel went back to bed, God did call again. "I'm listening," Samuel said to God. Then God told Samuel what He was going to do to Eli and his sons.

"I will punish them all," He said. "I have warned them about this."

Samuel stayed in bed all night. In the morning he opened the tabernacle doors as he always did. He was afraid to tell Eli what God had said. "You must tell me all that God said to you," Eli told Samuel. So Samuel told Eli what God had said. "God must do what He thinks is best," said Eli.

As the boy Samuel grew to be a man, people could see that God was with him. So they listened to Samuel. They knew that he would be God's prophet. God did give Samuel more messages. And Samuel told the people what God said.

# The Ark Is Captured

In a war between Israel and the Philistines, the Israelites were losing. So they retreated to talk. "Let's carry the ark of the covenant into battle," they decided. The ark was at the tabernacle at Shiloh.

So it was brought to the army camp at Ebenezer. Hophni and Phinehas, sons of Eli the priest, came with it and helped take it into battle. The Israelite soldiers shouted so loud when they saw the ark that they frightened the Philistines.

"The Israelite God has come to their camp," the Philistines said. "Fight harder than you have ever fought!"

The Philistines did fight harder. And they won. They even killed 30,000 Israelites and captured the ark.

One man escaped and ran to tell the old priest Eli the bad news. He was ninety-eight years old, blind, and fat. When he heard that the ark was captured and his sons killed in battle, Eli fell backward, broke his neck, and died.

The Philistines took the ark back to the temple of their god Dagon in Ashdod. The next morning they found Dagon's statue fallen down, with his face bowing to the ark. The next night the same thing happened, but this time Dagon's head and hands were broken off. Then a plague broke out in Ashdod.

The Philistines knew they were in trouble because of the ark. They decided to send the ark to Gath. When they did, the people there got the plague. They then sent it to Ekron, but the people there cried out against it.

At last the mayors of the five Philistine cities got together and urged the people to send the ark back to Israel. They were afraid of what might happen next.

# The Return of the Ark

For seven months the Philistines kept the ark of the covenant in their land. They had captured it from the Israelites, but it had brought them much trouble. Each city where the ark was taken had a bad plague.

At last the Philistine people were too afraid to keep the ark any longer. They called for their priests and sorcerers. "How should we return the ark to Israel?" they asked. "What gift should we send with it?"

"Send five golden tumors, like those we got in the plague," they answered. "And send five golden rats, like those that brought the plague. Put the ark in a new cart and hitch it to two cows that have new calves. Put their calves in a barn and these golden things next to the ark in the cart. Let the cows go. If they go to the Israelite city Beth Shemesh, you will know all this trouble came because we took the ark. If they stay here, you will know the plague came by accident."

The people did exactly as the priests and sorcerers said. The cows headed straight for Beth Shemesh in Israel, lowing as they went. The five mayors of the Philistine cities went as far as Israel.

The people of Beth Shemesh were harvesting wheat when they looked up and saw the ark coming. They were very happy. As the cart came into the field of a man named Joshua, it stopped near a big stone. The people broke the cart into pieces, built a fire, and sacrificed the cows as an offering to the Lord.

The five Philistine mayors watched a while and then returned to Ekron. They had sent the golden tumors and golden rats from their five cities—Ashdod, Gaza, Ashkelon, Gath, and Ekron.

# Saul Is Made King

Samuel became a great judge, a ruler over Israel. He was a good one, too, for he went from place to place, helping people know what God wanted them to do.

Samuel grew old and made his sons judges in his place. His sons, Joel and Abijah, ruled at Beersheba. But they were dishonest men and took bribes. At last the leaders of Israel had enough of this. They went to Samuel and demanded, "We want a king like the other nations around us." Samuel was upset and talked to the Lord about this.

"Warn them how a king will reign over them," the Lord said. But the people still wanted a king. Then the Lord told Samuel that Saul, the son of a wealthy man named Kish, would be king. Samuel took some oil and poured it on Saul's head. That was called anointing. It showed Saul and others that Saul would be king.

Saul was a tall man. Most people just reached his shoulders. When Samuel brought the people together and told them Saul would be their king, the people shouted, "Long live the king." Samuel told the people what they must do. He wrote in a book what the king should do and put it in a special place before the Lord.

Not all of the people were happy with their new king. Some troublemakers said, "How can this man save us?" They did not even bring their new king a present, as the others did. But Saul said nothing about it.

# Saul Sacrifices Wrongly

During his first year as king, Saul led his people to a great victory over some enemies. The people were sure now that he would be a strong king.

Saul kept about 3,000 of his troops together to defend Israel against the Philistines, a greater enemy than the one he had conquered. He set up camp with 2,000 at Michmash, while his son Jonathan took 1,000 and attacked some Philistines at Geba, destroying all of them. Saul called for the entire army to gather now, for the Philistines were angry.

But the Philistines gathered a much larger army. They had 3,000 with chariots, 6,000 on horses, and more than they could count on foot.

Now the Israelite soldiers became so afraid that they ran away. They hid in caves, among rocks, and even in tombs and cisterns. Some crossed the Jordan River to Gad and Gilead.

But Saul stayed with some trembling troops at Gilgal. Seven days earlier Samuel had told Saul to wait for him to come and make a sacrifice to the Lord. Samuel said he would be there in seven days.

Now Saul saw his men running away and decided not to wait for Samuel. He would make the sacrifice himself, even though he should not do that. Just as Saul was finishing, Samuel arrived.

"What have you done?" he asked Saul. "God told you what to do, and you have not obeyed Him. He will not let you or your sons keep on ruling as king. He will choose another who will obey Him." Then Samuel left.

# Jonathan's Bravery

King Saul had only 600 men left. The Philistines had thousands, with horses chariots and swords. Saul's men did not even have swords.

One day Saul's son Jonathan headed toward the Philistine camp with the young man who carried his armor. They had to climb up the steep wall of a ravine to get there.

"If the Philistines tell us to stay where we are, that will be God's way of telling us not to fight," said Jonathan. "But if they tell us to come up, that will be God's way of telling us to go and fight."

When the Philistines saw Jonathan, they told him to come up. So, Jonathan and his armorbearer climbed up the steep wall to the Philistine army camp. Suddenly the Philistines began to fight each other. Saul and his 600 men joined the battle, along with the men who had run away from Saul's army.

The Philistines began running from Saul's men. Then Saul made a foolish vow. "A curse on anyone who eats before evening," he said.

Jonathan did not hear what Saul said. So when they went through a forest, he dipped a stick into a honeycomb and ate some honey. When evening came Saul asked the Lord if they should keep going after the Philistines. But the Lord would not answer.

"We must find out what sin was done today," Saul said. "Whoever has sinned must die." Saul found out that Jonathan had eaten some honey. "You must die for this," he said. But the soldiers of Israel would not let that happen.

"Jonathan saved Israel today," they said. "He must not die." So they would not let Saul execute Jonathan.

# Samuel Anoints David

Saul was a good military man, leading his army to some great victories. But he was not the kind of king God wanted. Saul did not always obey God. Of course even a king needs to obey God. Samuel was sorry to see this happen.

"You have felt sorry long enough," God told Samuel one day. "Go to Bethlehem. I have chosen a son of Jesse to be the next king."

"Saul will kill me if he hears what I am doing," said Samuel.

"Take a heifer and make an offering there," God said. "When you do, I will show you which son is to be king. Then you can anoint him." Samuel did exactly what God said.

*This must be the one*, Samuel thought when he saw Jesse's first son, Eliab.

"No he isn't," God said. "You must not judge by appearance. I don't look at others that way. I look at their heart."

Jesse brought seven of his sons to Samuel. "God has not chosen any of these to be the next king," Samuel told Jesse. "Do you have any other sons?"

"The youngest is watching the sheep," said Jesse.

"Bring him here now," Samuel said. "We will not sit down until he has come." Jesse brought David, a good-looking young man with the well-tanned face of an outdoorsman.

"This is the one I have chosen," God told Samuel.

So Samuel poured oil on David's head while his brothers watched. Then God's Spirit came upon David.

# David and Goliath

The Philistine soldiers gathered between Suchoh and Azekah for a great battle. Saul gathered his Israelite army at the Valley of Elah. The Philistines were on one side of the valley and the Israelites on the other side.

One day a Philistine giant named Goliath came out into the valley. He was over nine feet tall, with a bronze helmet, a 125 pound armored suit, and bronze leg coverings. He carried a bronze javelin with a 16 pound iron head. His armor bearer carried a large shield for him.

Goliath shouted to the Israelites. "Send a man to fight me. If your soldier kills me, we will be your servants. If I kill him, you will serve us." Saul and his soldiers were afraid. They heard Goliath shout this every day for 40 days, twice each day.

One day Jesse sent his son David to the army camp with food for his brothers—Eliab, Abinadab, and Shammah, who served in Saul's army. David heard Goliath shouting and it made him angry. "I'll go fight this Philistine!" said David.

"All right, do it," said King Saul. "May God be with you." At first, Saul put his armor on David. But David could not walk. So he took five smooth stones from the brook and put them in his shepherd's bag. Then with his shepherd's staff and sling, he went to fight Goliath.

Goliath was angry that one so young came to fight this way. But David said, "I come to fight in the name of the Lord. He will conquer you."

As Goliath rushed toward him, David whipped a stone at Goliath with his sling. The stone sank into the giant's forehead, and he fell dead to the ground.

David grabbed Goliath's sword and cut off his head. When the Philistine soldiers saw that they ran. The Israelites chased them and won a great battle.

# The Friendship of David and Jonathan

Jonathan, son of King Saul, had watched as David went out to fight the Philistine giant Goliath. No other man would do this, and David was not even a soldier in Saul's army.

When David was brought to Saul, Jonathan admired him greatly. The two became close friends and developed a strong bond of love that day. Jonathan swore that he would be like a brother to David. To show that he really meant this, he gave David his robe, his sword, his bow, and his belt.

King Saul decided to keep David at the palace instead of letting him go home to Bethlehem. He made David his army commander. The soldiers were delighted that David would lead them.

But something strange happened the day David killed Goliath. On the way home some women came out singing and dancing with tambourines and musical instruments. They sang about David's killing ten thousands and Saul's killing only thousands. This made Saul jealous, for it gave more honor to David than to Saul.

"Now *what* more can he have but the kingdom?" Saul grumbled. So he began to watch David carefully.

# Saul Tries to Kill David

King Saul was jealous. After David killed Goliath, some women sang songs about David's killing tens of thousands while Saul killed only thousands. Saul wondered if the people would try to make David king instead of him.

The next day Saul was distressed. David played the harp for him, as he often did, to soothe him. Saul held his spear while David did this. Then suddenly Saul threw the spear at David, hoping to pin him to the wall and kill him. David jumped aside. This same thing happened another time. Saul became so jealous that he demoted David to captain. But this only made David more popular. David behaved wisely in all he did, and Saul became even more jealous.

Saul offered his older daughter Merab to David in marriage. But then Saul had her marry a man named Adriel instead. Then another of Saul's daughters, Michal, fell in love with David. Saul offered to let David marry her. "All you need to do is kill 100 Philistines," Saul told David. So David and his men killed 200. Then David married Michal.

When David became more popular than ever, Saul tried to get Jonathan and some others to kill him. But they wouldn't.

"David has always tried to help you," Jonathan told Saul. "Why should you try to kill him now?" For a while Saul did not try to kill David. But one day when Saul was listening to David play the harp, he threw his spear at him again and almost killed him. Then Saul ordered his men to kill David when he left his house in the morning. But Michal learned of this plan and helped David escape during the night.

# Jonathan Warns David

"Why does your father want to kill me?" David asked his friend Jonathan.

"But he doesn't," said Jonathan. He did not realize how much King Saul, his father, wanted to kill David.

"Your father would not tell you that he wants to kill me," said David. "He knows we are good friends."

"But what can I do?" Jonathan asked.

"Tomorrow starts the three-day feast of the New Moon," said David. "I won't be there. If Saul is angry, tell me and we will know he wants to kill me."

So Jonathan and David planned a signal. The next day David would hide by a pile of rocks. Jonathan would shoot three arrows nearby. Jonathan would send a boy after the arrows. If he told the boy that the arrows were on this side of him, David would know all was well. But if he said the arrows were beyond him, David would know Saul wanted to kill him.

On the third day of the feast Saul asked Jonathan about David. Jonathan gave an excuse that he and David had planned. Saul was so angry that he tried to kill Jonathan. Then Jonathan knew for sure that Saul wanted to kill David.

The next morning Jonathan shot the three arrows. When the boy ran for them, Jonathan called out, "the arrow is beyond you." That was the signal that Saul really did want to kill David.

When Jonathan sent the boy back to town with his bow and arrows, David came from his hiding place. The two friends shook hands and cried.

"Let's remember what we have promised," Jonathan told David. They were such good friends they had promised to be kind to each other and to each other's children as long as they lived. So David left and Jonathan went back to town.

# Abigail Shares Her Food

After Samuel died, Saul kept on hunting David, trying to kill him. He was jealous, afraid that David would become king instead of him. David had to keep moving around.

Once he came to the Wilderness of Paran. There a wealthy man named Nabal owned a sheep ranch near Carmel. As long as David and his men camped nearby, shepherds and their flocks.

One day, this man Nabal was at the ranch shearing sheep. He was a rude man with poor manners, while his wife Abigail was beautiful and intelligent.

David depended on men like this to feed him and his men as they wandered around, trying to keep away from Saul. So he sent 10 men to ask Nabal for food.

But Nabal was rude and insulted David and his men. So David left camp with 400 men to attack Nabal. While this was happening, one of Nabal's servants told Abigail what Nabal had done.

Abigail quickly gathered 200 loaves of bread, 2 jars of wine, 5 butchered sheep, 1 bushel of roasted grain, 100 clusters of raisins, and 200 fig cakes. She took these things on donkeys to David's camp.

David was still grumbling about Nabal when Abigail rode up with these things. She got off her donkey, bowed before David, and gave him the food.

"Praise God for sending you," David told her. "If you hadn't come, not one of Nabal's men would have been alive in the morning."

When Abigail told Nabal about this the next morning, he was so angry that he had a stroke. After lying there paralyzed for 10 days, he died. When David heard that, he sent for Abigail and married her.

# David Spares Saul

David had to keep moving around from place to place, hiding from King Saul. The king wanted to kill him because he was jealous and afraid David might become king.

Once when David was at the hill of Hachilah, the men from the Wilderness of Ziph nearby told Saul where he was. Saul took 3,000 of his best soldiers and camped near there. David's men knew all of this, for they had spies watching.

One night David and Abishai went down to Saul's camp. Saul and his general, Abner, were sleeping inside a circle of sleeping soldiers. David and Abishai slipped through these, until they came to Saul. "Let me kill Saul," said Abishai.

"No," said David. "God chose him to be king. God must take his life some day." David took Saul's spear and jug of water. Then he and Abishai slipped from the camp without anyone's knowing it.

When they had climbed safely on a mountain ridge nearby, David shouted. "Wake up, Abner!" he called. "Why haven't you guarded your king? Where is the spear and jug?"

Saul heard David and knew who it was. "Is that you, my son?" he called.

"Yes," David answered. "But why are you after me? What have I done wrong?"

"I have been wrong to chase you," Saul admitted. "Come home, and I will not harm you. You have saved my life today."

David gave Saul's spear to one of Saul's young men. Then David slipped away, and Saul went back home.

But David did not go home, for he did not trust Saul now. He knew that Saul might still try to kill him.

# Saul Dies in Battle

One day the Israelites and Philistines fought on Mount Gilboa. Many Israelites were killed. The rest ran away. Even King Saul and his sons tried to run away. But the Philistines caught them. They killed Saul's sons—Jonathan, Abinidab, and Malchishua.

The Philistine archers went after King Saul. They wounded him with their arrows.

"Kill me!" Saul told his armorbearer. "If you don't, they will torture me."

The armorbearer was afraid to kill his king. So Saul fell on his own sword and died. The armorbearer also fell on his sword and died.

The Israelites on the other side of the valley heard what had happened. They were afraid and ran away. Then the Philistines came and lived in their towns.

The next day the Philistines went to the battlefield to take things from the dead Israelites. When they found Saul and his sons, they cut off Saul's head. They took his armor, and sent word throughout the land that King Saul was dead.

The Philistines hung Saul's armor in the temple of the Ashtoreths. They hung his body on the wall of Beth Shan.

But brave Israelite warriors from Jabesh Gilead marched all night. They took the bodies of Saul and his sons back home and burned them there. Later they buried their bones under the tamarisk tree in town. Then they fasted for seven days.

# David Becomes King

After Saul died, David asked the Lord if he should go home to Judah. When the Lord said yes, David asked where he should go.

"To Hebron," the Lord told David.

David moved to Hebron, not far from his boyhood home at Bethlehem. He took with him his two wives, Ahinoam and Abigail. Some of David's friends also came with their families.

One day the leaders of Judah came to Hebron and made David their king. They anointed him, pouring oil on his head. This was the way leaders showed that the Lord was making someone king.

David was pleased that the people of Jabesh Gilead had buried Saul. He sent them a message. "The Lord will bless you, and I will be kind to you because you did this," David told them. "Now that Saul is dead, the leaders of Judah have made me their king."

Abner, commander of Saul's army, had taken Saul's son Ishbosheth to Mahanaim. The people there made Ishbosheth king over the rest of Israel. He was forty and ruled for two years. David ruled over Judah for seven and one half years.

# David Captures Jerusalem

One day some men killed Saul's son Ishbosheth. Then the leaders of Israel came to David at Hebron. "You are our king now," they told David. They anointed him with olive oil.

David was 30 at this time. He ruled for 40 years. He was king of Judah for seven and one half years. Then he was king of all Israel for 33 years.

After David became king of Israel, he wanted a new capital. Jerusalem was a strong-walled city. It was also called Jebus at that time. It would make a fine capital.

But the Jebusites already lived there. They were enemies. They thought David could not conquer it. "Even our blind and crippled men could keep you from taking this city," they mocked.

David sent his men up through the water tunnel. They captured the fortress of Zion. So this became David's new home and capital. He named it the City of David and built more around the fortress. He started his building program on the east side where the land was filled in.

The Lord was with David, and so he became stronger each day. Hiram, king of Tyre, gave David cedar logs, carpenters, and stone masons. David built a beautiful palace. He knew that the Lord was blessing him and his people.

When David moved to Jerusalem he married more wives and had more children. His children born in Jerusalem were Shammua, Shobab, Nathan, Solomon, Ibhar, Elishua, Nepheg, Japhia, Elishama, Eliada, and Eliphelet. Do you know anyone with any of these names?

# The Ark Is Moved

"Let's bring the ark of God to Jerusalem," David told his officers. They thought it was a good idea. So David ordered 30,000 soldiers to go with him to Kirjath Jearim. The ark was in a house there.

The ark was a beautiful golden chest that Moses had made in the wilderness. Inside were two tablets of stone with the Ten Commandments on them.

This day the ark was placed on a new cart, guided by Uzzah and Ahio. The ark had been in their father's home for many years. There was singing and dancing and music as the ark was taken to Jerusalem.

Suddenly one of the oxen pulling the cart stumbled. Uzzah grabbed the ark to hold it steady. But the Lord was angry at the way he did it. Uzzah dropped to the ground. He was dead.

David was afraid now and took the ark to the home of Obed-Edom nearby. There it stayed for three months.

One day David decided to try again. This time he had it carried the way God said. What a great time this was, with music and dancing.

At last the ark was placed in the tent that David had made for it. Then David and his people gave offerings to God.

David showed his thankfulness by giving each person there a loaf of bread, a piece of meat, and a cake of raisins. Imagine taking home special gifts from the king!

# Collect All 8
# Children's All-time Favorite Bible Stories

*Noah and the Great Flood*

*Moses Is Born*

*David and Goliath*

*Daniel in the Lion's Den*


*Jesus Is Born*

*The Good Samaritan*

*Jesus Is Raised from the Dead*

*Paul Sails and Is Shipwrecked*

www.ingramcontent.com/pod-product-compliance
Lightning Source LLC
Chambersburg PA
CBHW061800290426
44109CB00030B/2904